Millennial Melancholy

Nailah Nurse

BookLeaf Publishing

Presentation by *BookLeaf Publishing*

Web: www.bookleafpub.com

E-mail: info@bookleafpub.com

ISBN: 9789357442770

First edition 2023

*Dedicated to my son, Khari and to my family
for always pushing me and supporting any of
my endeavors.*

ACKNOWLEDGEMENT

To BookLeaf Publishing, for giving me the push to explore my inner thoughts and emotions and to be able to curate them into meaningful words to share with the world.

PREFACE

As someone who is extremely invested in the study of behavior and Childhood/Human Development, I find that a lot of us were sold dreams in our childhoods that many can now not afford.

In honor of healing my (and hopefully someone else's) inner child.

Unholy Union

My body is your temple
You should be worshipping at my feet
But instead you bring me offerings of anger, lies
and deceit
You sit in my pews to wreak havoc on my views
My choir sings their hymns but you drown out
their tunes
The trumpets blare and you sit there with an
impious glare
The preachers teach and you sacrilegiously stare
Adorers seeking atonement and glory
Seek to also add sanguinity to my spiritual
inventory
You sagaciously intrude upon my sanctuary
Sorry idolater, but your presence is temporary
Why refuse to depart?
Why choose to be a heathen operating with a
darkened heart?
You will never reach beyond these gates
From the shadows you can try to desecrate
But when the sun rises, you see everything it
illuminates

Grief is a Graveyard

Memories materialize only to die
Dark thoughts resurrected like zombies, come
alive
I bury my pain 6 feet under
Solidifying the soil with rich sadness
Uprooting the flowers with despair
Suffocated by pain
Grief is a cemetery where I pay my homage
again
I weep for what was and what could have been
Tears slowly erode the soil, seemingly
unearthing the corpses of my dreams
Pushing dark daisies and colorfully cremating
what once was
The ghosts of the past continue to haunt me
Grief is my graveyard and I visit this tombstone
daily

What to Do When You Forget To Water YOU

I woke up dead today …
Please don't be alarmed
But this is why self-care is so important
To deter us from this kind of self-harm
My leaves were browner than usual
Also noticed my flowers didn't look as beautiful
The soil was dehydrated, dry as dust
So I contacted my gardener, someone I can
really trust
Mentally retracing my steps, to see where I went
wrong
The roots laying hidden all along
We dug deeper, to uncover what I missed
My fragile life, delicately balancing on my
fingertips
We dug into the soil to get to the roots
And I realized, this is not something I can afford
to pollute
I have to remember to give back to ME
To reward myself, it doesn't cost much, it's
actually free
I can keep my plants from wilting with this one
simple rule:
In everything that you do, don't forget to water
YOU

Holistic Horticulture

My garden sprouted overnight
Now I spend my days nourishing the soil and
pruning my leaves
I was astonished when I began to achieve idyllic
growth where my soil was tainted
That I could sprout beautiful flowers that
mimicked a work of art, so vividly painted
As I grow, my garden grows
The vines tell me all the things I should know
The butterflies and bees pollinate my positive
thoughts, spreading it throughout my garden
My photosynthesis casually converting
optimism into carbon
A peasant at Demeter's will
My grass is greener and the land is still
But in the blink of an eye
My garden seemingly sprouted overnight

11:11

5

Angels mirror the good in this realm
Delivering mystifying messages when we feel
overwhelmed
These moments where you and the universe
synchronize
Are a connection to your subconscious in
numerical disguise
Auspicious interludes in the day
Seeing double not once, but twice displayed
A chance to wish upon a star
Or manifest under the moon
When the ticking of the clock becomes a
grandiose tune
A perfect pair
An intuition for the Lord's Prayer
An insight to prepare
A sense of enlightenment just in time for luck to
be "fair"

Sinful Symbiosis

Mistakenly aligned, forever intertwined
You go your way and I attempt to go mine
A magnetic field, void of gravity
Drawing us back to float through naivety
We were once a beautiful sunrise
Now our suns set on the horizon of lies
The ebb and flow of our rhythmic hearts
Yearns to crash on the shores to etch out the
part…
The part of you that needs
The part of you that grieves
The part of you that wants to release
Feel free if only for a moment
For we have become one
A sinful symbiosis

Stuporpowers

I can breathe in pain and exhale a miracle
I can call sailors to their watery graves with
something wicked and lyrical
I can convert dark days into sun rays
Turn my eyes into X-rays and set souls ablaze
I can bundle all my worries and make beautiful
bouquets
I can turn my troubles into loads of laundry
Sorting my degrees of despair
I can walk this earth turning pavement into thin
air
I can manifest my imperfections like shadows in
the light
I can darken the day and radiate the night
I can spark ideas that burn ever bright
I can validate my own soul like a parking meter
But even with all these *stupor* powers
I still can't defeat the Grim Reaper…

Eccentrically Egocentric

Supercalifragilisticexpialidocious
Living selfishly is my delightful diagnosis
Dying alone is the palpable prognosis
And if you say this loud enough you'll surely
sound precocious
The thought of it rather excites me
Not having to share my peace of mind with
anybody
Getting to wake up and make breakfast for one
While reading literature under the golden sun
At times I might miss someone to put sunscreen
on my back
But then I think of sharing someone else's
burdens and I'm right back on track
Your problems are yours, and yours alone
Which is probably why I watch notifications
accrue like debt on my phone
I care, but pain and sadness, I refuse to embrace
Egocentrically speaking, I strive to keep a smile
on my face
My delight in selfishness shines
With peace of mind as my prize

Ambivalent Adulting

Motivation woke me up this morning
It carefully shook me until I was awake
It made my bed, brushed my teeth and sat me
down at the table
Success made me a hearty breakfast packed with
vitamins and virtues
I fortified my meal with positive thoughts and
attainable aspirations
Then I washed it all down with a glass of
purpose
Destiny gave my agenda for the week with a
guiding hand
Urging me forward, reminding me of the plan
Though doubts may linger, my dreams pick me
up when I fall
And the Lord with his blessings, remains
through it all

How Sweet the Sound

Amazing grace, how sweet the sound
My transformation, wretched yet seemingly
profound
Trumpets blare, but there is only silence
There is no peace, emptiness acts as guidance
Floating aimlessly towards the void
Not sure if I want to be found, not sure if I will
be destroyed
The warmth of darkness can be comforting and
blinding
The pain and the incessant need, binding
Who wants to feel? Who needs to see?
Who wants to save a wretch like me?

Glitter Don't Mean Gold

All that glitters, is not gold
When you see me, think of the reaper that got
sowed
Imagine the barren land made fruitful once more
Imagine all the whispering souls, knocking at
my door
I *sore* above the world around me
I flutter, creating the illusion that they feel
lightly
But my wings are heavy
My past ain't pretty
I've reaped what I've sowed
And all that glitters, is not gold

Sabotaging the Simulation

We wake up, blink and we go from 3 to 30
Then comes the realization that you and death
will start to get flirty
Sensory overloaded by the thought of aging to
die
While perplexed by the thought that the desert
might actually be an alien hive
It has to be true!
I mean, I don't believe in Area 51 but a lot of
NPCs do
Did you hear our presidents are cousins?
And that the ocean is really space?
They say JFK was actually abducted by a UFO
without leaving a trace
There are 168 hours in a week, 40 of those we
are expected to slave
Just to sustain a life where only 1 was gave
No do-overs, no extra lives, no health boosts, no
cheat codes
A cleverly crafted deception we were all
randomly bestowed
This place isn't real, I can't help but highly
doubt
And when your simulation ends, they will plug
your computer out

Random Ramblings

I'm not as perfect as I portray
I started out empty, using others as a way
A way to feel superior emotionally
Flexing my manipulation and lack of sympathy
I championed self-control
While losing every battle to impulsivity
I highlight communication
But never the dark in me
I walk around not feeling the weight of the
world
Trying to adopt a carefree nature
But life's experiences burden your mind
Anchoring your essence, making it harder to
find
It would be naïve to continue with the mindset
I've followed for so long
But if we're being honest
It doesn't feel wrong
This might be my karma
I know I'm not a bad person
I'm just a selfish butterfly on the path to finding
what I deem as happiness
I am frightened by the very thing I am

Astounding Affirmations

I am loved, I am well respected
I am 128-bit encrypted password protected
I am versatile, I am the shift
If life is a present, I am the gift
I am the tree, I am the lift
I am a whiff
Of something sweet
My presence, my aura
A delightful treat
I am a breath of fresh air
A crown rests upon my head
My hair is an heir with its own royal flare
I am the wind beneath my own wings
I am worth more than ruby, emerald, sapphire
and diamond rings
The sun rises when I wake and sets when I sleep
There is no path I will take that will be too steep
Any journey that I begin, I will complete
My smile defies gravity
My touch can send chills right through your
heart cavity
I can turn insight into income
And with it, build a kingdom
My soul might be etched with pain
But supreme I shall always reign

COVID Cutie

15

Hey you there, with the N-95
I have been checking you out since the moment
you arrived
With your makeshift hazmat suit
And your rhinestone bubble-wrapped boots
Can we maybe stop and grab a Corona or 2?
Nah I'm just poking fun, I know there's nothing
to do
The world may be shut down but you have my
heart wide open
It's starting to feel heavier than this sack of toilet
paper I'm toting
I would love to watch our love blossom from an
epidemic to full on pandemic
A love so pure, so clean and so hygienic

My Grandad Gave Me This Coat

When I was born, I was told my grandad gave
me this coat
The coat always seemed so heavy
So bulky, like it didn't quite fit me
I refused to wear it proudly
Over the years, I tried to make my own
alterations
Reminding myself that one day I will soon have
my own self-liberation
My own coat, one that "looked good" and fit me
One that was easier to wear
But this coat? This coat was rare
This coat surely made people stare
I was unaware of the beauty of this coat
& the meaning behind this article of clothing
that I tote
The coat had meaning and purpose
The potential barely breaking the threaded
surface
"One who succeeds" he proclaimed to me
My granddad gave me this coat and I will wear
it proudly

Tender Touches

Tempted by the fruit of your soul
Warmed by the heat of your embrace
Enlightened with the intricate pathways of your
mind that lead me to the destination of your
heart's interface
Thank you for the sunshine on good days
And for being a shelter on bad days when it
rains
Even with the spiraling hurricanes of strife
Continuously beating me down in life
Your tender touches will always be a fortified
shelter throughout the night

Letter to my Lover

To the apple of my eye
The fruit of my loom
The sunshine above me that assists me in bloom
The light in my life that can brighten the darkest
room
You hold my flaws on a pedestal
And award me on bad days with shiny gold
medals
Love does not boast but allow me to rejoice
For diligent love is not a privilege, but a choice

Here's Two Haikus

19

1. The morning dew drip
   A sweet nectar on my lip
   Nature's blissful kiss

2. Emerald green eyes
   That whisper prosperity
   Viridescent gems

Happiness is a House

I crafted this home with my own two hands,
brick by brick
It's a work in progress, yet I'll never tire or quit
Some say it's a destination, a path or a route to
take
But for me, happiness is a small and cozy home
to make
With care and love, I shape it to feel just right
And it grows stronger, a symbol of my life's
delight
At times it might falter or even form a few
cracks
But with time and patience, it always bounces
back
A place of peace, my happiness abode
Where joy overflows, right through the windows
and out the door
For you and all the neighbors to revel and enjoy

Captain of Change

You are the captain of this vessel
Navigating through waters that like to wrestle
Steering the ship with a steady hand
You set out to change your life's plan
You stand at the helm and steer for your life
Your troubles docked back on the shore of strife
It's not quite often you set out to sea
Setting sail to break and feel free
Leaving behind all that you knew
A solo voyage with just you on crew
On your journey, do not stop nor bend the mast
Record a ship log if it will help you stay on task
Keep your focus, do not sway
And chart your course, come what may
If the water grows calm, your spirit will too
It will rise like dreams to skies, so blue
And whenever you start to lose hope
Remember that ships sink while dreams float

www.ingramcontent.com/pod-product-compliance
Lightning Source LLC
La Vergne TN
LVHW050250200726